Provence

An accidental gourmet's sketchbook
by John Davis

The Crowood Press

Acknowledgements

A lot of people have helped (and suffered) during the preparation of this book. These are just a few: John Burrows, who introduced me to Crowood; Patrick Collister, who warned me of the dangers of negative copy; David Gamble, for introducing me to Arles; Tim and Daška Hatton, for their photocopier, their fax and their advice on adjectives; Cathy John for her kindness and knowledge of book presentation; Pauline Larkin, for her encouragement and enthusiasm; John Larkin, whose boules trophy cabinet remains mysteriously empty; John Ryle, for withstanding the deafening sound of my typewriter; Jimmy Wormser, for his constant interest; Ian Wight, for our weekly literary luncheon. Finally, Charlotte Davis, without whom, as they say, this book would definitely not have been possible, and most of all Winni Olesen, who has suffered my endless moaning more than anyone else. I'm indebted to you all.

First published in 1994 by The Crowood Press Ltd, Ramsbury, Marlborough, Wiltshire SN8 2HR

British Library Cataloguing in Publication Data
A catalogue record for this book is available from the British Library.

ISBN 1 85223 843 7

Typeset by D & N Publishing, DTP & Editorial Services,
Crowood Lane, Ramsbury, Marlborough, Wiltshire SN8 2HR

Phototypeset by FIDO Imagesetting, Witney, Oxon

Printed and bound by BPC Hazell Books Ltd, Aylesbury

Typeface: Bodoni Book

Place Jean James - Grasse.

For Maggie and Brian Byfield.

It all began with a loaf of bread and a glass of wine. One bright August morning, sitting as usual with my friends around the table on our little terrace amongst the pines, I did a rough sketch of the remains of our breakfast baguette.

The previous day had seen temperatures hit the nineties, and judging by the yellow faces dominating the weather map on the back page of Nice-Matin, we were in for more of the same.

Even at this relatively early hour, any form of effort required instant refreshment, so I poured myself the first chilled rosé of the day. Having drawn the bread, I added what was left of the wine, and without knowing it, this book had begun.

My love affair with Provence started long ago, sometimes enticing me back three or four times a year, but in all that time I'd never once picked up a pencil. Like countless others I'd remained happy simply to sit back and immerse myself in this beautiful part of the world.

The sheer indulgence of an unforgettable dinner at a famous hilltop restaurant, or the magical discovery of a secluded olive grove, shimmering in the warm breath of late afternoon. The bustle and excitement of a village market, bathed in the dappled light of a tree-lined square, or best of all, observing life from the table of a pavement café, sipping pastis and letting the world drift by.

It wasn't until the following summer, back once again on the same terrace, that someone said I should think about a book.

I thought of the problems. I'd never written anything before and I didn't speak French. Most of us can get by within the safe confines of a bar or restaurant, but try making sense of a fast–talking stallholder with a thick Provençal accent and it's a different thing entirely.

However, I continued to draw. Simple compositions were followed by more complicated subjects requiring greater detail, leading me away from the house and into the village just over the hill.

Between drawings I decided to write down everything I could remember about my many experiences in Provence, going all the way back to a balmy night in the mid-sixties,

petit dejeuner, Bar Maryland – Le Muy.

emerging from the plane at Nice-Cote d'Azur airport and for the very first time breathing in the wonderfully exotic blend of salt, pine resin and aviation fuel.

Then I began placing things together geographically, village by village, town by town and quite unintentionally at first, restaurant by restaurant. (I hadn't realized how great a part they played in so many memories.)

Whilst there's much more to Provence than just food and drink, the simple, free-spirited cooking of this vibrant region has always been one of the main reasons for it's lasting popularity. We've always been led to believe that the great artists were lured to this area because of the quality of light. I'm sure they were, but I bet it wasn't the only reason.

Provence is the home of many great chefs, but it also contains many more unsung heroes, happily preparing dishes from time-honoured recipes in surroundings that have escaped the attentions of tourist guides.

A New Year's Eve dinner at Roger Vergé's famous moulin in Mougins was fabulous, but then so was a Boxing Day lunch at a down-at-heel place called The Pony Bar, just outside Nice.

I spent the entire afternoon behind a mountainous platter of Moules-Frites, forever being topped up by the more than generous patron whilst the world and their dogs, all festively over-dressed, danced between the tables to the accompaniment of a greasy old juke-box. Ask me which of the two meals I preferred and I'd be hard-put to answer.

I began to discover places further afield and the different days on which markets were held. I learnt about the seasons and what to look for; the arrival of tiny courgettes in mid-May and the celebrations heralding the garlic harvest in August and early September. On the way I picked up the odd recipe, some of which I've included. Sometimes my sketchbook took me back to places that held many fond memories, only to discover that memories were all that remained. The panoramic auberge overlooking

Sunday market – Le Muy.

Pain de campagne – Draguignan.

Pegomas, where we used to eat spit-roasted rabbit and knock back as many pichets as we liked, all for a set price, had burnt down and never re-opened. On the other hand, the sleepy village of Trans-en-Provence, with its ancient bridges and cascading springs, now boasted a marvellous boulanger, who bakes traditional Pain-au-Levain in a wood-burning oven housed in a back-street cellar.

There were many such experiences, and that really is what this book is all about. An affair that's lasted nearly thirty years, filled with fond memories and new discoveries.

I hope it gives some impression of what life is like in this brilliant corner of France, where the sky can stay blue from April to December, and buying a loaf of bread sometimes takes all day.

Le Bosquet, April 1994.

Le Muy is our nearest village. It sits on a wide plateau of vines at the edge of the Massif des Maures, between the town of Draguignan to the north, and the coastal resorts of Sainte-Maxime and Saint-Tropez.

Since I started these drawings, it has undergone development of staggering proportions, but for the moment at least, its heart remains more or less the same; to a passing traveller, little more than another sleepy spot on the map. Unless, that is, it happens to be Sunday, for this is market day.

Every village has its regular stallholders, who rarely change. Le Muy has its own garlic man, Monsieur Julius Caesail (clearly a connoisseur of the dreadful pun). During the summer he swaps his pre-war flying helmet, complete with goggles, for a Roman crown of garlic entwined with bay-leaves.

Next door, in the shadow of the old church, his partner sells salt cod, anchovies and numerous varieties of olives from blue plastic washing-up bowls. On the opposite corner you can buy warm brown eggs, or if you can endure the performance in rescuing one from the cage, a chicken to lay them for you.

Further down amongst the mobile garden centres, army surplus and audio cassette stalls, vibrating discordantly to the strains of Johnny Hallyday and Sylvie Vartan, you find huge mountain hams and rocky chunks of grey Pain de Campagne.

Velvety Bries and tiny Crottins de Chavignol are placed on vine leaves and displayed in glass cabinets surrounded by bottles of locally pressed olive oil.

On the site of the ancient pissoir, the pitfalls of the democratic system are broadcast via megaphone by a Jean-Marie Le Pen supporter distributing neo-fascist literature, and in the smoke-filled Bar Maryland, the patron laments the performance of the national team in the previous night's match, with a gendarme, propped against the bar. In the window, a group of Algerians in dark turbans play cards, clattering plastic

chips on the formica table and in the corner, oblivious to it all, the old brown and white Boxer drifts in and out of sleep on a bed of yellow cigarette ends and unsuccessful lottery tickets.

Meanwhile, on the bottom corner, inside the busy maison de la presse, the locals animatedly discuss the morning's news, as reported in the colourful pages of Nice-Matin: more fires, yet another fatal pile-up, the never ending list of births, deaths and marriages. And quite often – something peculiar to the French – bank robberies of the most daring and spectacular nature.

I was once told that about two hundred years ago, the French government issued a decree, supposedly for the well-being of the people, stating that every town or village, no matter how small, should have its own bakery. If this is true, then it's something with which Le Muy has more than complied.

Stand at the top of the square and within view are no less than four boulangeries. Add to these

another four in the surrounding streets, two more in nearby alley-ways and yet another in the supermarket on the ringroad encircling the village and this makes a grand total of eleven — surely some kind of record, even for France.

From the same viewpoint there are also three butchers, the best being Monsieur Henry, who like his predecessor Monsieur Basso, sells not only the finest cuts of meat, beautifully presented, but also makes his own delicious casseroles and cannelloni.

His only serious rival used to be five miles away in Puget, where you found an inordinate number of

male customers carefully eyeing Madame Pallavisini, a young Stéfane Audran, as she expertly filleted and deboned their purchases. Her husband,

Hommage à Madame Pallavisini.

whose impressive collection of rugby trophies decorated the shelves, kept an equally close eye on the customers.

By mid-morning the temperature reaches the high seventies and a crowd gathers at the church as a very young bride and groom nervously appear, blinking in the bright sunlight. As the clock strikes eleven (and again at five past, for some reason), the first smells of Sunday lunch in preparation begin wafting out from first floor windows overlooking the market; basil from the Soupe au Pistou; garlic and thyme from the Courgettes Farcies; fennel and saffron from the Bouillabaisse.

If it happens to be October, chestnuts from the Ardêche, or even closer from the woods around La Garde-Freinet, are a welcome addition to fruit and salad stalls. Fried in olive oil and paprika, they make a great accompaniment to chicken, or even better, added to a Salade Frissée aux Lardons.

In the crowded patisserie, lemon and apricot tarts are delicately placed in thin boxes and tied with ribbon, to be offered as a traditional lunchtime gift, along with the last-minute purchase of an extra baguette to alleviate the national fear of being caught without a loaf.

At twelve o'clock the hooter goes and things begin winding up. The two little gypsy girls lead away their

Charcuterie — Le Marais.

troupe of baby goats, used to attract the crowds to their display of 'Bonbons Resineux'; herbal lozenges with supposedly medicinal attributes.

You really do get the feeling of the circus leaving town. The unfortunate chickens are bundled squawking into the back of a baking hot corrugated van and the man selling truly brutal hair clippers takes a farewell nip at the neck of a straggling punter. (I once saw him destroy an entire family's hair, leaving the husband watery-eyed as the result of a surprise attack on his ears and nostrils.)

Kitchen gadgets and combat outfits are hurriedly packed away and as the police begin dismantling the barricades, the mobile pizzerias grind their way out of the square into the Route de la Bourgade.

Within an hour it's all gone. Everything. Not the slightest clue to what's gone before, and not a soul to be found anywhere. Just the occasional sound of a well-tuned Volvo, speeding its occupants towards the sea. Le Muy is once again, sleeping.

The restaurants are of the honest, no-nonsense variety found throughout France. Les Jonquières offers standards such as Jambon de Montaigne and Daube Provençale, as does Le Vieux Piano, along with Tripes Marseillaise. In the rustic surroundings of the Abreuvoir, Terrine de Sanglier and a number of charcoal-grilled dishes are served in a farmyard setting overlooked by red rocks and parasol pines.

The food may lack sophistication, which isn't a criticism, but the wines of this region are definitely on the up, mainly as a result of a greater understanding of modern production methods by the proprietors. Just outside the village at La Motte, Domaine de Saint Roman d'Esclans have started winning awards throughout France for their reds, the Cotes de Provence Couvée Special being their super smooth front runner. It won't be long before Domaine Valette in Les Arcs do the same, again for their reds.

A few miles away at Chateau L'Arnaud between Vidauban and Lorgues, H.J. Knapp, a former architect fairly new to the business, is producing rosés full of fruit that compare favourably with the better known Domaines OTT (an appropriately named wine if ever there was).

Domaine de Saint Roman d'Esclans.

As an Englishman, I always associate roast lamb with Sunday lunch, a tradition we keep up in Provence, albeit a little later in the day. (After a gruelling morning at the market, a few reviving Pelforths in the Bar Maryland are hard to resist.) The basic recipe for Gigot Boucher or Gigot Boulanger has been attributed to butchers and bakers all over France, so I dedicate my own particular version to Monsieur Henry, the smiling butcher of Le Muy.

GIGOT BOUCHER (for 6 to 8 people)

A little olive oil
6 medium sized potatoes, thinly sliced
4 onions, thinly sliced
4 large tomatoes, thinly sliced
8 courgettes, finely chopped
6 garlic cloves, crushed or chopped
A handful of fresh thyme • Salt and pepper
A large leg of lamb

Pre-heat the oven to maximum. Drizzle some oil over the bottom of a deep roasting pan. Arrange a layer of potatoes, onions and then tomatoes in the pan. Sprinkle some of the courgettes, garlic and thyme over the top and season with salt and pepper. Continue to layer and season in the same way, making sure you end up with potatoes on top.

Trim all but a thin layer of fat from the lamb and put it on a wire rack in the centre of the pan, to allow the juices to run evenly over the gratin. Drizzle a drop of oil over the lamb and the gratin, season with salt and pepper and roast for half an hour. Reduce the heat by half and cook until the lamb is done the way you like it. Remove from the oven and let it stand for ten minutes. The gratin will stay hot in the pan.

As well as the wonderful climate, the scenery and the food, there are a few less attractive things I automatically associate with Provence, the most predictable of these being the power cut, the blocked drain and the hangover. This remedy for the latter was given to me by the man who came to unblock the waste pipe, and I've included it because it actually works! (You can increase the amounts depending on the number of casualties.)

AIGO BOULIDO (for 1 person)

2 large garlic cloves, peeled • 1 sage leaf (it's essential you use fresh herbs) • 1 bayleaf
1 sprig of thyme • Salt and pepper • A few slices of bread, cut thin and toasted
Enough olive oil to cover the bread

Place the garlic, sage, bay-leaf and thyme in a saucepan containing half a pint of water. Bring to the boil, add salt and pepper and continue boiling for 10 to 15 minutes. Heat the oil and place the toast in the bottom of a soup bowl. Pour the oil over the bread, and then the hot water, removing the herbs but leaving the garlic. It'll be soft and help clear your head. A la votre!

In the hills above Nice, at the end of a gently climbing road that winds upwards from the coast, is the little village of Saint-Paul-de-Vence.

Once upon a time a man called Paul Roux opened a café here called the Robinson. His mum did the cooking and they lived in a tiny room out the back.

Paul married a young girl called Titine and very soon they had a son, Francis. The café did well and before long they added a few tables outside and planted trees to shade them from the sun.

They re-named it La Colombe d'Or and it became popular with the many artists and writers working in the area, and soon the café turned into a restaurant, and finally an hotel.

In his spare time Paul used to paint, as well as collecting pictures painted by some of the customers. People like Braque, Chagall and Picasso.

As they grew older, Francis took a more active role, always aware of the sympathetic principles of his parents. He in turn got married and after Paul and Titine retired, he and Yvonne took over the hotel, which they and their children have now run for many years.

What started out as a simple roadside café is now one of the most famous and best loved hotels in the world. I first stayed here over twenty-five years ago and whilst the atmosphere was probably more tranquil, and

Les Hors d'Œuvre 140
Colombe d'Or
avec la charcuterie

the view from the terrace much greener, my feelings haven't really changed.

When you open the thick olive wood door, the huge marble dove nesting in the ivy above, you enter a protected domain. La Colombe d'Or, home of the family Roux. And unlike any other hotel I know, it becomes your home too.

During summer, lunch is served on the terrace, a sea of pink tablecloths and beige parasols, surrounded by fig trees. To begin, you're presented with a menu only just smaller than the table, each dish scrawled across the double page in Matisse-like handwriting.

It's really quite clever. Nothing on the menu ever seems to change — and nobody wants it to. I doubt if anyone knows who the chef is, and given the ingredients, most of the dishes you could probably prepare yourself. Which is also quite clever, as home cooking isn't something immediately associated with hotel cuisine.

There's nothing dull about a plate of Parma ham if it's the best you've ever eaten.

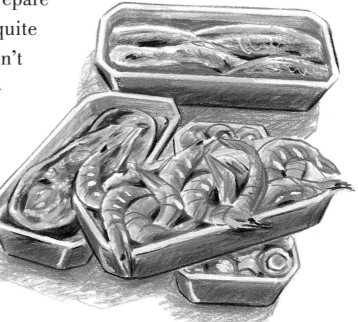

The same applies to the massive selection of hors d'œvres, where the creative role is played by the waiter in managing to fit everything on the table.

First to arrive is a wicker basket filled with artichokes, tomatoes, celery, radishes and hard-boiled eggs. Then the building work begins. This takes the form of a Lego style construction of oblong dishes, each placed with considerable dexterity allowing just enough space in which to slot the next. Herrings, anchovies, sardines, stuffed courgettes, caramelized onions and much, much, more.

When this culinary condo is finally built, the waiter bids you 'bon appetit' in a tone suggesting that your lunch has now been declared officially open.

Fernand Léger, that most graphic of artists, used to eat at La Colombe d'Or. Set in the wall separating the terrace from the outside world is one of his largest ceramics, 'Les Feurmes du Perroquet' made nearby in Biot. There can't be many recognized works of art displayed in such cheerful surroundings. A hefty iron mobile by Alexander Calder creaks gently at the edge of the olive-green pool, where reflected in the water is a glittering dove mosaic by Georges Braque.

Metallic sounds of a different kind can be heard from the direction of the square, which as in most villages, serves as a general meeting place and the area designated for boules.

The commonest version of this magnificent game is called Pétanque, an abbreviation of 'pieds tanqués', or 'feet tied together', and for anyone who's never fully understood the rules, I'll explain them.

It's played on almost any surface except grass, and the rougher the terrain, the more skilful it becomes, as the person who reads it best has the advantage.

Playing combinations consist of either one against one, two against two or three against three. In singles and doubles each player has three

The bouledrome – St. Paul de Vence.

boules, but in triples, only two. (However, in a singles match it's more fun to play with six each.)

The game starts with the toss of a coin and a player from the winning side draws a circle between 35 and 50 centimetres in diameter. Standing in the circle he or she throws the wooden cochonnet a distance of between 6 and 10 metres. You really need a playing area of at least 4 metres by 15, as if the cochonnet lands less than about half a metre from the boundary this requires a re-throw.

The same player then throws or rolls a boule (knuckles uppermost) as close as they can get to the cochonnet. Then someone from the opposing team tries to place a boule closer, by either rolling or hitting the other one out. If this is achieved it's then the turn of the opposition to do the same.

If they fail to get closer, they keep throwing, which may mean using up all their boules and still not doing so. This leaves the other team free to score further points with their remaining boules. At the end of each round, one point is scored for each boule that is closer to the cochonnet than the nearest of the opposing team. The winning team starts the next game from the other end, and the overall winners are the first team to reach thirteen points.

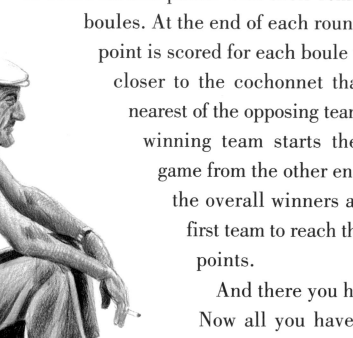

And there you have it. Now all you have to do is get hold of a set of boules, begin drinking a little earlier in the day, and – if not already hooked – start smoking. (During play, the dedicated boulist smokes only untipped brands, usually Gitanes or Gauloises Caporal, but if you insist on being a wimp, Craven 'A' cork tipped are tolerated.)

There's another type of boules also played in St-Paul, known as 'jeu Provençale'. It involves a running throw over a greater distance, and was the forerunner of Pétanque. This is the game I associate with Yves Montand. His love for St-Paul, La Colombe d'Or and the game of boules began in the fifties when he married Simone Signoret in the village church and held the reception at the hotel, something imitated by countless others since.

From that day, the hotel became his home too. I can't remember many summers when he wasn't around, an ever pleasant man, passionately in love with Provence. Now he's gone the place is like a theatre without its leading player.

I remember watching a game between Montand and his great friend Lino Ventura, who was also a regular and another of my cinema heroes. One had driven a lorry load of nitroglycerine through hell and high water, the other had staged the greatest jewel robbery the Cote d'Azur has ever seen, yet here they were arguing about the distance between two metal balls and a bit of wood.

At one point Lino looked up for a second opinion and I saw in his tired eyes someone for whom these moments were of great importance. The image remained with me for the rest of the holiday. When I got back home I was told he'd died a few days later.

On another occasion I was sitting outside the café, where once again Montand was playing a game with the boys. The bus pulled up, bringing the kids back from school and when they saw who was playing they began to disrupt the game. Montand sent them packing into the bar by bribing them with an offer of free drinks.

Moments later a perplexed waiter appeared at the door and shouted across the terrace in the direction of the players. 'Monsieur Montand? They've all ordered champagne!'

St-Paul is never boring. You can dip in and out of the summer circus as your mood takes you, without getting stuck on the tourist merry-go-round.

All it takes is a short stroll.

Down the hill from the hotel is one of the nicest art galleries in France. The Maeght Foundation was the conception of gallery owner Aimé

Painting by Miro in the dining room
of La Colombe d'Or – St. Paul.

Maeght, back in the mid-sixties. Bonnard, Matisse and Mirò are all represented, whilst Giacometti has an entire terrace named after him, where spindly bronze figures are dotted around like underfed chess pieces on a giant board.

What they'd make of the village's current artists-in-residence is better left unanswered. These denim-clad Dufys will happily hold forth with laughable self-importance to any punter prepared to listen, predictably culminating in a cordial invitation to accompany them to their studio in order to view their creations first-hand. Whereupon the subject abruptly changes from post-modernism to post anything anywhere (just sign the Amex slip).

Early evening in the bar of La Colombe d'Or. In an alcove is a picture of grand'mère Titine, taken in the same spot. I remember her sitting with her little white dog by the entrance, greeting the rich and famous with a slight nod of the head. I always felt she wasn't particularly interested in who they were, knowing only too well they knew exactly who she was!

It's a bit like an up-market bar-tabac, where the next to arrive might be today's latest media guru, or yesterday's 007. In the dining room anniversaries, awards and movie deals are celebrated amongst the Bonnards and Picassos. (Years ago a gang of art thieves stole the entire collection, later discovered crated-up ready for departure at Marseille railway station.)

Over the years, many households have sold out to the merchants and galleries that dominate St-Paul, some not relishing the thought of their homes

forming the backdrop to a million videos, others preferring the comfort of high-rise living in the suburbs of Nice and Cannes. However, as far as I know, one person who has resisted all such offers can still be found at another St-Paul institution. La Hostellerie de la Fontaine is not La Colombe d'Or. Its plumbing compares with the noisiest in France, its ceilings have been about to collapse for a hundred years, and like the person who runs it, it is very old – and utterly charming.

One Christmas, a group of us were sitting eating croissants in the dingy breakfast room, the air rich with the aroma of coffee and burning paraffin, as Madame la patronne scanned the Christmas Day edition of Nice-Matin.

She put the paper down and came and sat next to us. In a sad reflective tone she told us that over the years she'd seen five husbands buried, and adopting a child-like pose said how very lonely she always felt on Christmas Day.

Of all the times spent in St-Paul, this is the day I remember most fondly. The whole of France was caught in the grip of a major freeze-up. Snow had fallen the previous night, covering the village in a white blanket and making it look from a distance like a drunken wedding cake.

It didn't seem to bother the boules players though, play continuing as usual even when cochonnets were barely visible. I wondered where their wives were, or whether a life dedicated to boules precluded any possibility of marriage.

Former residents returned to see what the old place looked like in the snow. By turning things upside-down, nature had unwittingly offered me the opportunity to see life in St-Paul as it must have looked half a century ago. Inside the crowded café, warming armagnac replaced pastis, and children made portholes in the steamed-up windows.

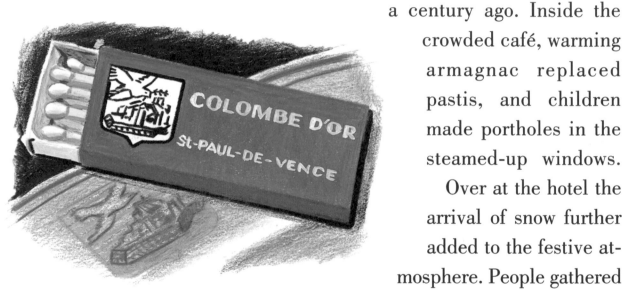

Over at the hotel the arrival of snow further added to the festive atmosphere. People gathered earlier than usual at the bar, many suffering from the effects of the previous night. Monsieur Roux, wearing a bright new cashmere number by La Coste, whistled as he organized the lunch bookings. His son François, slightly dishevelled as usual, listened to the explanations of the staff, many of whom were late because of the weather.

Still wearing his white summer shoes, the local taxi driver took messages from a mobile phone, and above the general din of crashing cutlery, someone in the kitchen sang an aria from La Bohème. I'm sure Paul and Titine would have approved.

Close to the village on a quiet stretch of the Route de Cagnes is a little restaurant called La Strega. On a pretty shaded terrace Gilbert Stella varies the menu in accordance with what's best at the market. One day a perfectly steamed lotte, another, a delicious rabbit paté served 'en croute', and when in season, courgette flowers stuffed with a lotte and basil mousse.

Just above St-Paul, the town of Vence is probably best known for its Matisse chapel and near-by, the stunning Chateau Saint-Martin. Where the avenues Alphonse Terreille and General Leclerc meet, a flight of steps leads to a rather serious looking restaurant, Le Vieux Couvent, that is, in fact, quite friendly once the formalities are dealt with.

Complimentary bites are a great invention as they let you know what you're in for. If they're bad, you know to keep it simple. If they're good, as when I was presented with what can only be described as a lump of bread pudding filled with crispy bacon, they can lead to your ordering the full Menu Gourmand.

The foie-gras sits on top of green beans surrounded by tomato. The fillet of beef is cooked with red wine and shallots, served with a brilliant egg and potato scone.  Grilled chèvre has a dollop of acacia honey poured over just before serving (an inspired idea as I didn't like either before) and contrasts

perfectly with the bitterness of the rocket salad.

Dishes like this represent culinary life at its most appealing, as two noble uniforms join ranks. The farmer, dressed in traditional bleues de travail, and the chef, resplendent in spotless whites, working hand in hand, each dependent on the other.

From Vence, the road leads to the artistic village of Tourrettes-sur-Loup, where many houses contain studios at ground level. Even the children can often be seen selling their own, less contrived creations. The two gendarmes of Tourrettes watch over the square, eager to issue 'un papillon' (so named because it flutters on your windscreen) to any motorist daring to park out of line.

Backstreet - Tournettes-sur-Loup.

In the hilltop village of Biot, beneath the arches of the Place des Arcades, there's an hotel restaurant that for as long as I can remember, has produced basic, authentic Provençal dishes at their best. The Café des Arcades is always lively, whether it's a miserable February lunchtime or a sweltering summer night, when its a good time to order the Salade Niçoise.

There are countless versions, but it really depends on how filling you want it to be. Some idiots will scream at the inclusion of potatoes, others will adamantly defend it. In this one, you'll find it substantial enough to serve as a main course.

SALADE NIÇOISE (for 5 or 6 people)

For the salad
2 tins of tuna fish (in brine not oil)
1lb french beans, cut in 2 inch lengths, boiled 'al dente'
2lb small waxy potatoes, boiled, skinned, halved and kept warm
4 tender celery stalks, sliced ¼ inch thick
1 green and 1 red pepper, seeded and sliced ¼ inch thick
4 large tomatoes, peeled, seeded, cut in 1 inch segments
3 free-range eggs, hard boiled, each cut into four
1 tin of anchovy fillets • A large handful of black oil-preserved olives

For the dressing
3 garlic cloves, minced • 9 or 10 basil leaves, cut into thin strips
¼ pint of olive oil (first pressing) • Salt and pepper

In a large bowl, flake the tuna with a fork and add all the other ingredients except the eggs, olives and anchovies. In a smaller bowl, mix together the garlic and the basil, stir in the oil and season with salt and pepper. Pour over the salad and gently mix the ingredients. Place the salad in a long shallow dish, decorate with the eggs, criss-cross with anchovies and dot with olives.

On Fridays the village of Le Luc holds a market that stretches beyond the square and into the maze of streets surrounding it. Hidden in the woods behind the hamlet of Flassans-sur-Issole is a terrific hotel restaurant called La Grillade au Feu de Bois, or quite simply, The Charcoal Grill. It's a common restaurant name in France, but rarely is it associated with somewhere of this quality.

While you contemplate the short menu on a terrace shaded by fig trees, Roman urns and a riot of geraniums, Germaine Babb will appear to discuss the day's specialities. The stuffed sardines are a permanent fixture, and this is the recipe as I recall it.

SARDINES FARCIES (for 6 people)

1lb spinach • 1 onion, finely chopped • 6 tablespoons of olive oil
2 tablespoons of flour • 6oz of ricotta cheese • 3 garlic cloves, minced
Salt and pepper • A handful of rosemary • 2oz of dried breadcrumbs
18 sardines, scaled, gutted, heads and backbones removed, tails left on

Tear the spinach leaves from their stems and wash clean. Cook in boiling water for about 4 minutes until tender. Rinse in cold water, drain and finely chop. Soften the onion in hot oil, add the spinach and continue to cook for a few minutes longer, then stir in the flour.

Spoon in the cheese and garlic, and season with salt and pepper, stirring vigorously for 5 minutes until thoroughly blended. Remove from the heat and sprinkle with rosemary, mixing well. Stuff the sardines with a spoonful of the mixture each and roll them in breadcrumbs. Place side by side in an oiled baking tin and bake in a hot oven for about 10 minutes, till brown. (Alternatively they can be deep-fried, in which case they'll only take a couple of minutes.)

I don't know if it was just the sound of the name, but before I ever came to France I always pictured Antibes as a quiet little port with a few fishing boats, which every so often held a jazz festival.

Well, there are two ports, one of them very old, and I'm sure there must be one or two fishing boats hidden somewhere amongst the thousands of gleaming white yachts that cram the moorings of the Vieux Port and the Port Vauban from May until mid September.

In fact, Antibes is a bustling town, where the area surrounding the Place du General de Gaulle could easily pass for a warmer arrondissement of the nation's capital.

Like Paris, streets with names such as Wilson, Foch and Verdun bear witness to two world wars, but despite this Antibes retains a happy, gentle feeling. (Even the centre for martial arts advertises itself as being non-violent.)

There are several museums, a French version of Marineland and some nice shops, making it the sort of place not reliant on good weather to be enjoyed. Personally, I've spent many a pleasant hour in the huge librairie-papeterie by the square, which like a lot of French bookshops has a vaguely clinical feel.

LIBRAIRIE-PAPETERIE

We've still got a lot to learn in this area. Why is it, for instance, that in the average provincial French town you find ten times the amount of international magazines on sale than you do in London? In this particular shop you find everything from Billboard to The Lancet, and authors ranging from J.R.R. Tolkien to J.R. Hartley.

The town's exotic past is reflected in the goods on sale in parts of the covered market in the old quarter. As well as the usual mixture of fifties frocks and incomprehensible T-shirts you find kaftans, turbans, incense-burners and fly-swats.

Though essentially a Provençal market, many of the herbs and spices have more in common with those found in the markets of Athens and Istanbul. For anyone craving a curry, the key ingredients can be found here.

It was also in Antibes that Picasso cured my hangover.

I'll start again. After a night that began with dinner at a smart place in Juan-les-Pins, La Terrasse, and ended in a pub run by Tynesiders somewhere in the market district, I awoke knowing the only way I'd get through a day in which the sun was rising with considerable venom, meant finding somewhere quiet to hide. Surprisingly I found the answer in a guide book which began as follows: 'The works on display in the Picasso Museum

include many he painted in the cool, spacious rooms set aside during his stay in Antibes …' So off I set, head thumping.

The Grimaldi palace overlooks the bay from the ramparts enclosing the old town. It stood abandoned for years before being turned into a museum devoted to the history of the town and its environs.

At the end of 1946 Picasso met the curator, who offered him the upper floor, his own studio being not big enough for the paintings he was planning. For the next few months he worked on what became known as his 'Antipolis' series, this being the town's original Latin name. These enormous pictures with their dancing fauns and centaurs became the museum's main attraction and led to it being renamed after the artist.

Nevertheless, it was going to take more than these to take my mind off my present condition. But then, for the first time, I saw the ceramics. Row upon row of the most beautiful plates and vases. And the colours! Jugs and bowls in tones of incredible subtlety. Plates painted in bold strokes that sang out at me.

The story goes that in later life Picasso became increasingly depressed that his neighbour Matisse never once came to see what he was up to, whereas he often called at Matisse's studio to do just that. He needn't have worried. Picasso loved the colours of Provence, as did his contemporaries, but if you appreciate the difficulties of using ceramic

pigments, you begin to see he understood those colours more than any of them.

As I wandered from room to room, every so often I caught a glimpse through the fortress windows of the view across the bay. It was staggering. The Mediterranean had turned pure silver under the high sun, and the little ferry boats heading for Ste-Marguerite formed bobbing silhouettes on the breeze. Even the doves, that hover as if in homage to the man who drew them so often, looked grey in comparison.

Inside, I saw all kinds of animals. Some engraved in brown or white clay, then painted and glazed, others shaped into fat vases or thin-necked decanters. What they all had in common was an overt feeling of celebration, something that he found hard to suppress. Perhaps it's me, but I've always found something cheerful even in his most tragic subjects.

Two photographs spring to mind. One shows Picasso sitting at a table holding up the skeleton of a fish he's just eaten. In the other, he's pressing it into a lump of clay, the start of another ceramic. His attitude to art, and way of expressing it are summed up perfectly.

These pieces left such an impression that when I got back to London I joined an evening class, only to discover that what had looked simple, wasn't, and that in order to make ceramics that looked like Picasso's, you had to be Picasso.

He said that in reality he used few colours, but what

gave the illusion was in putting them in the right place. He was referring to his paintings, but the point is best illustrated in this radiant, totally uplifting collection.

And so it was, that 23 paintings, 33 drawings, 27 lithographs, 2 sculptures and 78 ceramics later, I walked out of the Musée Picasso into the blinding light, not merely elated, but with a completely clear head. If proof of the man's genius were ever needed, this was more than enough for me.

A few years ago, a friend of mine rang to see if I fancied a spot of lunch the following week. The slight problem being that I was in London and he was ringing from his hotel in the South of France. How I managed it is another story, but I did, and I'll never forget the experience as the restaurant was the Eden Roc, and the hotel was the Grand Hotel du Cap.

I arrived straight from the airport and late for lunch. As I climbed the marble steps carrying a plumber's bag containing a dozen heavy boules making a terrible clunking noise, it didn't take a genius to see this wasn't the sort of place where we were likely to find a few old boys in carpet slippers, sipping pastis and eager for a game. As I walked past the reception I hoped I might be mistaken for the maintenance department, but I wasn't smart enough, and the only old boy I could see was Kirk Douglas.

However, no one batted an eyelid (at least not so you'd notice, they're so well-trained) and I made my way down to the restaurant at the water's edge. My friend was waiting and we both laughed, and after a few glasses, settled down to a large grilled loup de mer and I began to feel at home.

Apart from being one of the world's most exclusive and expensive hotels (it's only open seven months of the year and they don't take plastic) it may well be the most beautiful. It sits on the tip of the Cap d'Antibes in eight hectares of manicured parkland. From the terrace you see on one side the lovely Esterel mountains and on the other, the Mediterranean and the islands of Ste-Marguerite and St-Honorat.

From the restaurant it looks like Buckingham Palace, seen from the Cenotaph, but with its pale yellow façade and ocean-grey shutters, much smarter. I've been back a few times now, as you don't have to re-negotiate your mortgage to have an evening drink on the balcony, which is the best time to go. The only sound you'll hear is the distant 'bop' of tennis balls from the discreetly hidden courts, and around seven o'clock the streetlamps on either side of the path turn everything into a scene from *Tender Is The Night*.

Even in this rarified atmosphere the staff may join you for a chat. On one occasion a waiter began showing me pictures of his kids and of the house he was in the process of building. The subject moved on to tennis. He asked if I played and I said badly. I asked who his favourite player was and not surprisingly he said Yannik Noah.

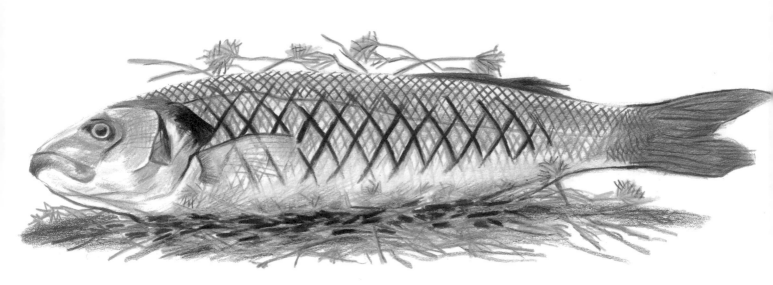

Also situated on the Cap is one of the best fish restaurants in the world. The Bacon is run by the Sordello brothers and the fact that they seem to have access to varieties of fish nowadays rarely found in the Mediterranean is seen in some envious quarters as in itself a bit fishy.

One thing's for certain, if you ain't had Bouillabaisse at the Bacon, you ain't had Bouillabaisse. The waiter flings a large bib over your head in the manner of an old-fashioned hairdresser before serving this delicious creation straight from the pan. It's quite amusing to see a table of adults, dressed up like babies, supping away contentedly from silver spoons. (Given the prices here, it helps if you were born with one in your mouth.)

Despite being basically a simple fisherman's stew, it's not necessarily that easy to do properly. Each fish must be dropped in the boiling stock in order of consistency. Get this even slightly wrong and you've blown it.

Just outside Antibes is Jo Rostang's famous Bonne Auberge, now run mainly by his son Phillippe. The suburb of La Brague isn't the most attractive of places and the restaurant doesn't gain much by being trapped between the main road and the railway, but I wouldn't mind being there now.

From the outside it's like a Mexican hacienda, an impression that's

given added spice by the colourful ladies who patrol this bushy, broom-lined section of the Route Nationale, touting for business.

Inside, the atmosphere is of a restaurant that knows it's the bee's knees, yet despite the lavish surroundings retains an air of informality.

There are two things I associate with this place. First, the Gratin Dauphinoise is not made on the premises, it comes straight from heaven, and second, for anyone who enjoys a

bit of table theatre, it's essential to order something involving the employment of the duck press. This gleaming silver mangle is expertly manoeuvred alongside your table, whereupon knobs are twisted, catches released and handles lovingly turned until the last dribble of goodness is wrung from the carcass, then flambéed to make gravy for your plateful of Canard Sauvage.

But my favourite restaurant in Antibes is unlikely to pick up any stars, even though the food is as good as in many of the Côte's decorated temples. It's just as well this part of the Rue Republique is a 'zone pietonne', as L'Oursin

would hardly catch the eye from a passing car. Even on foot you could easily miss it. At first glance it's just another fish shop, and it's only when you realize that huge tin trays, strewn with seaweed and shellfish, are disappearing inside, that the possibilities of its being a restaurant occurs to you.

Most days, by 12.30 the place is packed with people so over-French they look like a job lot sent straight from central casting. They're mostly quite old and all accompanied by at least one dog, but often two or three. (Dogs are a frequent feature in this book, not because I'm particularly fond of them but because the French are obsessed with them.)

In places like this you feel naked without a quivering poodle or foul-tempered dachshund to shout at. Hardly a moment passes without a yelp from under the cramped tables, where for the umpteenth time poor Chou-Chou fails to avoid the foot of a hard-pressed waiter.

The staff look like old snooker players and the tables are covered in what were once brightly coloured cloths, their descriptive motifs faded by years of laundering.

Even in France, Coquilles Saint-Jacques can be a hit-and-miss affair, but here they're perfect; breadcrumbs just crisp,

creamy and tender beneath. Moules come in a sticky cream and shallot sauce, but retain their brinish flavour.

On the ground floor there's a swing door that serves as a monument to Jacques Tati. To negotiate it the waiters require the movement and precision of a Swiss watch, something they all seem to possess. As the door swings back, it's booted the other way giving the waiter just enough time to make it through to the dining room. When the swing is completed, it's kicked back the other way by the next waiter returning to the kitchen, and so it goes on. In addition, the door answers back with an unconnected 'bonk' of it's own, just like the one in the hotel where Monsieur Hulot spent his holiday.

I used to stay in a village called Pegomas, at an hotel made up of apartments, each with a tiny kitchen area. I remember spending a morning in the market in Grasse and coming back to prepare a Soupe de Poissons for the evening. That night, as we sat on our terrace, boxed in by a low privet, residents poked their heads over the hedge to see where the smells were coming from, somewhat surprised that an Englishman was attempting their most sacred dish. I felt quite pleased by their response upon being offered a taste, especially given the equipment provided.

SOUPE DE POISSONS (for 7 or 8 people)

For the soup

¼ pint of olive oil • 1lb of onions, sliced • 1 bulb of fennel, chopped • 2 leeks, split and chopped
1 head of garlic, unpeeled, cut in quarters • 6 large tomatoes, chopped
3lb mixed white fish, gutted (if possible include some eel) • 3 sprigs of thyme (or 1 teaspoon of dried)
2 bayleaves • 2 or 3 tablespoons of tomato paste • A strip of dried orange peel
½ small wine glass of pastis • ½ teaspoon of saffron strands • Salt and pepper

For the Sauce Rouille

2 small chillies (fresh or dried) • 6 garlic cloves, peeled • 3 egg yolks
5 tablespoons of olive oil • 2 teaspoons of tomato paste • 1 tablespoon of fish soup

For serving

Thin French loaf cut in ½ inch slices and toasted • Gruyère or Emmenthal cheese, thinly grated

Preparing the soup

Heat the oil in a large saucepan, add all the vegetables except the tomatoes and cook over a medium heat until soft. Add the tomatoes and the fish and continue cooking for about 5 minutes. Add 7 or 8 pints of water. When this has boiled, add all the remaining ingredients except the saffron. Continue to boil for about 45 minutes, topping up with water if necessary. Away from the heat remove the largest bones and puree the contents through a food mill or processor.

Pass everything through a sieve, pressing firmly with a wooden spoon or pestle. Return the soup to the saucepan, bring to the boil, add the saffron and simmer for a further 15 minutes and season with salt and pepper.

Preparing the sauce

Crush the garlic and chillies in a bowl, or preferably a mortar. Add the egg yolks and dribble in the oil, stirring continuously until a thick mayonnaise is formed. Stir in the tomato paste and a tablespoon of soup and pour into a small serving bowl.

Serving the soup

Pour the soup into a tureen, passing the cheese and toasted croutons around separately.

Our Pegomas kitchen contained no oven, so all the cooking was done in either a large frying pan that would wobble uncertainly on the cylinder-fed hob, a collection of saucepans that had clearly done service in the Foreign Legion and a trumpet-like mouli-legumes resembling an early gramophone (even more so when the hotel dog came visiting, usually around meal times). Still, the lack of complexity in Provençal cooking meant most things were achievable and this highly colourful fry-up is a good example, rich in flavour, yet simplicity itself to prepare.

POULET PROVENÇALE (for 6 people)

12 chicken pieces • ¼ pint of olive oil • 10 shallots, finely chopped
4 large garlic cloves, finely chopped • Salt and pepper • 2 teaspoons of paprika
4 teaspoons of tomato paste • 2 tins of tomatoes, pressed through a sieve or passed through a
mouli-legumes • 1 red, 1 green and 1 yellow pepper, cut in halves and then in ½ inch slices
2 bayleaves • 1 large sprig of thyme • 1 sprig of rosemary • A handful of parsley, finely chopped
½ teaspoon of saffron strands • 2 glasses of white wine • A cup of black olives, stoned

In a large frying pan, sauté the chicken pieces in the hot oil until well browned. Lower the gas, add the shallots and sauté until golden. Add the garlic and season with salt, pepper and paprika. Combine all the other ingredients apart from the wine and olives and cook slowly for 10 minutes, then add the wine and cook for a further 45 minutes (if it begins to stick, add water or a drop more wine). The resulting sauce should have a thick, soupy consistency. Stir in the olives, cook for a further 30 minutes and serve straight from the pan.

Though not particularly Provençale, boiled potatoes mashed with butter and some of their cooking water go well with this dish.

Some of the most famous French films of the 30s and 40s, including *Les Enfants du Paradis* and *Quai des Brumes* contained sets designed by Alexandre Trauner, whose cobbled streets and crooked shop fronts suited the theatrical style and dramatic scenarios that were all the rage.

All this came to mind the evening I first saw Mougins.

Tall buildings in the square cast black shadows in the moonlight. Beneath, candle-lit restaurants glowed from within and in the centre a delicate fountain gurgled merrily. If Trauner and Franco Zeffirelli had joined forces, Mougins would have been the result. You could fit the entire village into a large film studio, and although I've been back many times, I still get the feeling that when I leave, the set is broken, the ivy boxed up with the fountain and it's all sent back to the warehouse to await my return.

The fact that this tiny place is known throughout the world is entirely due to one man – Roger Vergé. In his younger days he worked in hotels and restaurants from Paris to Casablanca. In Nairobi he ran kitchens supplying airlines with inflight

meals, winning contracts with airports throughout Central and East Africa. But in 1969, when he took over an old olive mill just outside the village, Mougins was about to be put on the map.

The following year he won his first Michelin star. In 1972 he won another and was awarded the medal of a 'Meilleur Ouvrier de France'. Now he has a third star. As well as all this he has interests in many other restaurants including one in the Epcot Centre in Florida, a café in Monte-Carlo and his name appears on wines, foods and books the world over. Not bad when you consider all he ever wanted to be was an aviation mechanic.

His restaurant, called Le Moulin de Mougins, is situated in the leafy quarter of Notre-Dame-de-la-Vie (where Picasso spent his final years, and Jaqueline eventually committed suicide). To the right is a boutique selling pâtés, confitures and anything else from which the enterprising M. Vergé can make a buck. The bar area houses the original press from earlier times, and the dining room is filled with antique furniture and copious arrangements of flowers.

I came here once on New Year's Eve, and it's not something I'm likely to forget. Though not officially a black tie event, we'd decided formal dress would add a note of celebration. Seated, somewhat flatteringly, at an enormous round table in prime position, we watched the other people arriving. Six women appeared dressed in obscenely expensive furs, clearly upset at being asked to shed them before being shown to their table. They were not the only ones, and by the time the meal got going, the entrance had begun to look like Crufts.

What followed ran to a mere nine courses, but such is Vergé's dexterity at playing one dish off with the next, none of us came out of it groaning. I kept the menu, so I can tell you exactly what we ate – napkins ready?

Pâté chaud de Lièvre aux Airelles; Fines Belons au Vinaigre de Vin; Petite Saucisse à l'Aneth; Le Ballottin de Saumon frais juste fumé en Mousseline d'Ecrevisse et les grains de Beluga; La Nage de Homard Breton en coulis léger de Truffes noires du Vaucluse; Le Granité de feuilles d'Estragon au Vin de Paille; Les tendres Filets de Poule faisane d'Alsace et la Crépinette de Cuisse aux Choux verts, Sauce Sublime; Le Foie-gras frais des Landes en gelée de Coing et sa Navette briochée; And finally, Tous les Desserts et les Gourmandises de la Saint Sylvestre. Happy New Year! (As dishes were still arriving well after midnight, you could say this meal took two years to eat.) After dinner, my friend's wife asked if she might be allowed to thank the chef personally for what had been a fabulous evening, so Christian, the charming manager, took her off to meet Roger Vergé. Eventually she returned, followed by the chef, and the entire dining room rose and gave him a standing ovation for what had been a memorable occasion.

In the centre of the village, Vergé's other main flagship is L'Amandier, a tall ivy-covered building with interiors that rival the Moulin. Chefs have come and gone, but I'll never forget the Apricot Gratin when Francis Chauveau ran the kitchen. Pure sex.

However, my favourite restaurant is just across the road. Monsieur Ballatore and Monsieur Giordano have been in charge of Le Bistrot for years, and despite its constant success, the friendly welcome and romantic charm remain the same, as does the menu.

The only part on ground level is the kitchen. I once stood at the open window as the chef (watched closely by a greyhound) chopped leeks at such speed you hardly saw the blade. Behind him on a shelf was an old black and white TV showing a football match. God knows how he still had all his fingers, as whenever the crowd noise increased, he swung round to look, but carried on chopping.

The dining room is in the cellar and has been left in its original format, retaining the stone walls and arched ceilings. Whilst much of the room is lit by candles, the wall lights are ingeniously simple, hidden behind roofing tiles pinned by iron supports. I've had virtually everything on the menu, including the Pieds et Paquets (lambs trotters and stomach, stuffed with bacon and herbs).

But it was through eating one of this restaurant's specialities that I ended up at the doctor. Friends of ours were staying down the road and I went to meet them the morning after I'd been to the Bistro. All night I'd been bothered by what felt like a tiny bone in my throat, which by morning had started to swell up.

My friends rang a local doctor and I drove down to his surgery on the outskirts of Mouans-Sartoux. A uniformed nurse ushered me into a room where the doctor was waiting. He looked like a character out of a Raymond Chandler novel, one of those shady types who whilst putting up a respectable front are secretly pumping some crippled general's daughter with something nasty.

Tall and thin, aged about sixty, with pale blue eyes, bleached hair and an immaculate sun-tan, he bore a striking resemblance to the actor Christopher Plummer. On the wall was an original painting by Edward Hopper. Having laid me out on the couch he stuck a lever with a mirror on the end down my throat, and peered into it with the aid of a silver torch. Whilst doing this he asked a series of questions that were not easy to answer coherently, given my predicament. Which restaurant had I been to? What did I have to eat? And so on.

Half gargling I said I'd eaten at the Bistro and had the Filet de Rascasse with anchovies. He paused for a moment before exhaling. Then, climbing further inside so our faces almost touched, he whispered in a tone you only associate with the gravest medical questions: 'Tell me … how was the sauce?'

Only in France.

He never retrieved the bone, but thanks to a tube of jelly that froze everything from my shoulders up, I ended up OK and I dare say I'm still carrying a small part of that dinner around with me today.

Those with sharp eyes might spot a sign, just off the square, leading to the hotel Mas Candille, where we once came for lunch on what was supposed to be the last day of our holiday. There aren't many hotels that can boast such a stunning view: from the terrace you look out across a fertile plateau, the distant hills turning paler shades of blue in the summer haze.

Time was running out, but the impending gloom of an airport check-in wasn't something any of us could contemplate with any degree of enthusiasm. Perhaps just one more bottle might pull us round. Of course, it had the reverse effect. At the time we were due to take off, we were still on the terrace, merrily toasting the planes as they rose in the sky from the direction of Nice.

We stayed the night, not wanting to spoil our self-awarded bonus, and for anyone plagued with fears of missing their flight, let me recommend it. It's the most wonderful form of therapy.

Every summer, a French friend of mine, who lives in Dorset, goes back home for the family re-union in Mougins. The time I was invited his dad organized a boules tournament followed by a celebration dinner of bread and cheese, and an enormous kettle of Soupe au Pistou. I'll never forget that night, seated around Mammie and Pappie's table in the middle of an orchard, telling jokes, singing songs, accompanied from the shadows by a choir of amorous frogs and toads.

SOUPE AU PISTOU (for 8 to 10 people)

For the soup

½lb haricot beans, soaked for 12 hours, drained • 1 bouquet garni (thyme, parsley and bay-leaves)
Salt and pepper • 12 small courgettes, cut in ½ inch slices • 6 carrots, peeled and sliced
10 leeks, with some of the green, split and chopped • 6 tablespoons of olive oil
2½lb of green beans, cut in 3 or 4 pieces • 4 tender celery stalks, thinly sliced
1 large onion, chopped • 6 tablespoons of olive oil • 5oz of pasta shells
3 chicken stock cubes, or 1 pint of home-made stock • 3 medium sized potatoes, peeled and diced

For the Pistou sauce

4 large garlic cloves, peeled and chopped • 25 to 30 basil leaves • 1 cup of Parmesan cheese, grated
5 large tomatoes, peeled, seeded and chopped • 5 tablespoons of olive oil

Preparing the soup

Put the haricot beans in a large saucepan with the bouquet garni and enough water to cover well. When boiled, add salt and cook for about an hour until the beans are almost soft, then set aside. Put all the vegetables apart from the potatoes in an equally large stewpot, add the oil and cook over a medium heat for 8 to 10 minutes. Pour in 7 or 8 pints of water, add the stock and bring to the boil. Add salt and simmer for 20 minutes. Add the potatoes and the pasta and continue simmering for a further 20 minutes. The soup should be fairly thick, but don't be afraid to add water if you think it's needed.

Preparing the sauce

Crush the garlic. Tear the basil leaves from their stalks and add to the garlic. Pound until they form a paste, add the Parmesan cheese, the tomato and mix thoroughly. Slowly add the oil, mixing until everything's blended together.

Serving the soup

Remove the bouquet garni and add the beans, with their liquid, to the stewpot. Bring back to the boil, then away from the heat, stir in the sauce and serve immediately.

The soup was made by André's mum, but his own speciality is the French answer to Italy's favourite snack, Pissaladière. On a winter's night in Stour Provost the table has often been warmed by the arrival, straight from the oven, of this sunny dish. Served with a simple green salad and generous supplies of red or white wine, it's the perfect supper dish.

PISSALADIÈRE (for 7 or 8 people)

For the base

¼oz of fresh yeast (found in most healthfood shops)
8oz of unbleached flour • 1 egg • 1 teaspoon of salt

For the filling

3 tablespoons of olive oil • 6 medium sized white onions (they're much milder)
1 teaspoon of thyme, finely chopped • 1 teaspoon of rosemary, finely chopped
Salt and pepper • 2 tins of anchovy fillets
A handful of fleshy black, oil-preserved olives

Preparing the base

Crumble the yeast into a cup of warm water and leave for 6 or 7 minutes until dissolved. Sift the flour into a mixing bowl, making a well in the centre. Pour the dissolved yeast into the well, along with the egg and the salt. Mix thoroughly, adding a little extra flour if necessary, until it becomes doughy. Place it on a floured surface and knead for 10 minutes, until it becomes elastic. Shape into a football and place in a large oiled bowl, rolling the dough so the surface becomes oiled. Cover with a damp cloth and leave for about an hour until risen.

Preparing the filling

Heat the oil in a pan and add the onions and herbs, and season with salt and pepper. Cover the pan, reduce the heat to very low and cook for 20 minutes, stirring occasionally.

To complete the Pissaladière

Take the dough, squeezing out any air and press flat in a 12 inch circular baking tray (or oblong tray of roughly the same area), pressing the dough up at the edges. Spread the filling over the dough, criss-cross with anchovies and press the olives between the diamond shapes. Leave for 15 minutes and then bake in a fairly hot oven for about 20 minutes until the dough is crisp.

There are few historical references in this book and it's quite deliberate, as I don't think the highlighting of ancient conquests or fastidious dating of changes in architectural style are of much help when describing life in present day Provence. Also, I've always found history a bit boring. I remain to this day one of those poor unfortunates whose knowledge is based largely on what Hollywood taught me.

However, it's impossible to write about Arles without at least a nod to the past, which has left an indelible mark on the town; a crumbling old theatre in which life is played out against an ancient backdrop, where the unwary visitor may begin as one of the audience, but may very easily end up one of the players – for this place has mysterious powers. For most of us, dreams of a home in Provence usually centre around an old farmhouse surrounded by vineyards and olive groves, and not the heat and noise of city life. But

such is the power of the spell that Arles can cast on the innocent bystander. It happened to a friend of mine. A couple of years ago he won a European photographic competition and was invited to Arles for the prizegiving. Within months he'd bought a house, and now spends every available moment there.

I arrived at his new home late on a baking hot afternoon, a tall medieval building hidden in a maze of streets so narrow that houses built on opposite sides almost touched at the roof-tops. Inside, the stone walls suppressed all sound other than that of a flamenco guitar, its gentle rhythm filtering across from an upstairs window (I'd yet to learn of the town's strong Spanish influence).

Later on as darkness began to fall, we wandered up to the centre for a drink and emerging from an alley into the light of a thousand overhead bulbs, we arrived in the Place du Forum, the Ancienne Place des Hommes, and at that moment, something I can't begin to explain, touched me too.

We found a seat at a bar on the corner and watched the waiters dart between the tables opposite, where each bar has a plot distinguished by different coloured parasols. It took some time to take everything in. A couple of doors up stood Van Gogh's 'Café de la Nuit', its façade restored in the colours of his painting, alive with laughter and activity, and at the far corner dominating the square, the Hotel Nord Pinus. From a first floor window a pretty girl lounged against the wrought-iron balcony from which hung the crooked hotel letters and at the window above, another pegged underwear on a line strung across the open doors.

I'm now of the opinion that Arles contains more beautiful women than anywhere else in France, most of whom were parading up and down the Forum that night. I was introduced to what became a regular drink, the gaily coloured pastis 'tomate', to which you add a shot of grenadine, which like many sweet tasting drinks can prove dangerously deceptive.

The poet Frederic Mistral was born outside Saint-Rémy, and

perched opposite the hotel his larger-than-life figure, a cross between Colonel Sanders and Buffalo Bill, looks down on the evening revelry. The speciality at most cafés in the Forum is either Paella, or Saucisson de Toro, made from the black bulls bred locally in the Camargue.

There's an extremely cheeky young mime artist performing in this square. He lies in wait at the nearest table, his whitewashed face studying the posture and mannerisms of unsuspecting tourists. Having chosen a victim he casually creeps up from behind and joins in their footsteps, exaggerating their expressions. People are left bewildered as to why they've become the centre of attention. He's quite possibly the first mime ever to have made anyone laugh.

But the impromptu star on this particular evening was a young girl who brought the Forum to a standstill with a provocative dance solo, accompanied by a guitarist who turned out to be one of the Gipsy Kings.

Later on, and now fully under the spell, I walked up past the Nord Pinus (where a few years ago, Helmut Newton photographed Charlotte Rampling

sprawled naked across a bed in one of the rooms) and into the Place de la Republique. On the southern side is the church of Saint Trophime, its 12th-century portal looking rather spooky in the borrowed light from the town hall opposite.

Poking out of the fountain in the middle is a crooked Egyptian-looking obelisk that was originally discovered on the site of the ancient circus. It looked a bit like I felt at the end of my first night here, rather wobbly and slightly the worse for wear. I made my way home past darkened restaurants, where upturned paella pans stood chained end to end. Shutters clattered down on all but the most exotic of bars. On reaching the house I remember wondering how long this rather strange attraction for the place would last.

In the week that followed, each day brought new discoveries. I walked the streets passing through different ethnic communities, each with their own distinctive sounds and smells, the contrasting food shops a testimony to the old town's colourful history as a major trading centre.

Van Gogh's association with Arles stems largely from his prolific output over what was, in fact, an incredibly short period of time. What's even more surprising is that for most of the time his health was very poor (at one point he was close to death), he suffered from wild delusions, he cut off half his ear, spent time isolated in a hospital cell, yet in only 444 days managed to produce around 200 paintings (including the 'Sunflowers' series) and over 100 drawings. When I think how long it's taken to produce this book, I'm embarrassed.

He died virtually penniless, but if one was to calculate the combined value of these paintings at today's prices, then divide it by the time he spent producing them, it would be interesting to see what his day-rate would have been.

The arena is by far the most imposing epitaph to the Roman occupation of Arles. Built during the 1st and 2nd centuries, only two tiers are left intact, but during the festival season the crowds still pour in. Strolling through the dark passages reminded me of my first visit to Wembley, the difference being that at the end of each section there are what look like large mouseholes, through which half-starved lions once chased the scent towards the pitch.

Arched prison cells, barely visible in the dim corridors brought back memories of celluloid martyrs of a bygone era; Victor Mature, Anthony Quinn and the bravest gladiator of all – Kirk Douglas.

My companion on this rare cultural diversion was a rather sorrowful dog that appeared from one of the alcoves, looking somewhat ashamed at being the most ferocious beast the arena could offer. Climbing to the highest level out into the light I looked down to where Caesar's

slaves received their final address: 'Those, who are about to die, we salute you.' It still retains an aura of cruelty, as chilling today as ever.

Restaurants and cafés trade off the arena, forming a circle around the perimeter. At one such place I noticed a party of Americans, identified by their badges as a Christian fellowship from Peoria, Illinois. As they attempted to decipher the menu it crossed my mind that 2,000 years ago, they'd probably have been the plât du jour.

I'd arrived in Arles during the photographic festival which included a retrospective of work by the British photographer Don McCullin. Elsewhere in town they were holding a festival of fourth-rate Italio-American historical epic films, the 'Festival du Film Peplum', an expression coined by a French critic which has something to do with the daft costumes.

We trooped up the Boulevard des Lices into the Theatre Antique on the opening night and took our places on the marble terrace, under a sky full of stars more brilliant than any we were about to see on the screen. The film was **Land Of The Pharaohs** made in 1954 by Howard Hawks, and it concerns the obsessive desire of the King of Egypt (played in true RAF style by Jack Hawkins at his most uncomfortable) to build the pyramids as burial vaults for himself and his successors. He forcibly enlists the help of a half-blind architect (James Robertson Justice, still thinking he's Sir Lancelot Sprat) with the promise of freedom. However, he falls for the charms of the Cypriot ambassador (Joan Collins – no description necessary), which leads to his downfall, whilst she ends up buried alive in the pyramids.

Most of the cast are overweight and therefore required to deliver their lines holding their stomachs in, adding a somewhat pent-up note to many exchanges. Nevertheless, the audience sat captivated, many of the hilarious exchanges lost in the French sub-titles. But when warned of the dangers in leaving Alexandria open to Joan's scheming, Hawkins commands his lieutenant: 'Saddle me two of your fastest camels!' people began to get the message and by the end, the old theatre was rocking with laughter.

We strolled back through the gardens, littered with Romanesque debris and out again onto the boulevard, stopping for a drink outside the Brasserie Waux-Hall. Next door there's a McDonald's you could almost call 'smart-chic', with trendy aluminium tables and spacious atmosphere. A few doors down is the Souleiado fabric shop, its windows radiating with the colours and traditional costume patterns of Provence.

On Saturdays this wide boulevard is transformed into one of the largest open air markets in the south. It stretches the entire length, beginning at the top in the Boulevard des Ramparts selling plants and flowers, down to the junction with the Rue Gambetta, where it changes from a food market into a clothing bazaar selling patterned skirts copied from Souleiado originals. Like the Forum, this market has more than its fair share of pretty girls. In most markets, they're usually found at the flower stalls, but here you're just as likely to see an olive-skinned face framed between a row of well hung saucisson as you are popping up among the gladioli. I suppose the best known product on sale here is Saucisson d'Arles. It's made with roughly 75% pork and 25% beef (or sometimes donkey) to which is added garlic, paprika and lardons, giving it an added substance. Then it's simply hung out to dry till ripe. With the odd regional exception, most of the produce can be found in other markets south of the Durance, but there's just more of it here. Goat's cheese from Banon, each tightly wrapped in a chestnut leaf, purple and white figs from Carpentras and freshly picked melons from Cavaillon. The shopping list is endless.

A less pleasant addition to the butchers' stands during

festivals are the decapitated heads of fighting bulls, killed in the arena. I witnessed this bloody spectacle when I returned the following Easter, a holiday period when a substantial proportion of the town is drunk for the best part of a week.

This time I saw the arena as it must have looked in Roman times – thousands of excited people jostling at turnstiles and charging through the outer galleries before spilling out onto the terraces. My previous companion was nowhere to be seen. The atmosphere was like a pagan cup final as cheers went up at the announcement of those taking part in the Corrida. The loudest accolade went to a stunning blonde girl called Marie-Serra, a home-grown star whose initials appear branded on the backsides of designer jeans sold in her boutique near the arena. (I doubt whether the prominent 'M & S' would have quite the same cachet back here.)

The overwhelming sense of drama as these brave and brilliant performers rode into combat with what are without doubt the most dangerous things on four legs, cannot be denied. But by the time I'd seen a dozen or so of these creatures taunted and bled into submission I'd had enough. Any moralizing on my part would be hypocritical, as I must have been responsible for the deaths of several thousand oysters, and having watched geese force-fed with corn to swell their livers (which really is a ghastly business), I'm still tempted by a plate of foie-gras. Neither could be deemed essential to my nutrition – I just like them too much.

Leaving the arena close to the tradesmen's entrance I watched as two men wearing overalls staged a mock sword fight with long Sabatier knives. At which point the horse-drawn cart carrying the dead bulls from the arena appeared. Within a minute the bull had been hauled onto an overhead hook, beheaded, disembowelled and hosed down. Then a refrigerated lorry bearing a butcher's motif screeched to a halt under the arch, its engine still running as the carcass was bundled aboard, then hurriedly driven away, no doubt to reappear on the menu in the Forum at a later date. Three ambulances were reverse-parked outside the players' entrance. Though not needed on this occasion they bore more than adequate testimony to just how dangerous this sport can be – for all those taking part.

The Hotel d'Arlatan is situated in one of the town's oldest, and certainly narrowest streets, the Rue Sauvage. The building dates back to the 1400s but it wasn't until 1920 that it was converted into an hotel, which has now been in the same family for four generations. Today it's run by Yves, Colette and Roger Desjardin, known to all as 'Monsieur Roger', along much the same easy going lines as La Colombe d'Or.

Nothing ever seems to be too much trouble for Monsieur Roger, who'll often be seen buzzing round the streets astride an old moped, saddle bags slung over the back, looking more like the village postman than the owner of the best hotel in town. Breakfast is served on a shaded patio that forms part of the courtyard. The rooms are immaculate, and like everything else, decorated with great taste and subtlety.

At the bottom of the Rue Forum there's a little place hiding under a vine-covered

Guido — the best chef in Arles.

conservatory called the Poisson Banane, which I hope takes its name from a fish and not a recipe. The set-price menu offers a variety of soups followed by Lamb Cutlets, Stuffed Tomatoes and Tarte au Pommes, all perfectly cooked, something borne out by the large family groups who eat here. A pichet of local rosé suits both the food and setting.

But the best restaurant in Arles is Le Médiéval, just behind the Forum in the Rue Truchet. This place represents everything a restaurant should. Honest cooking in a welcoming atmosphere where immediately you feel at home. Where the kitchen is as clean as the dining room and ingredients arrive for your inspection beforehand (something many restaurants wouldn't dare do).

This feeling of well-being is all thanks to Guido Balistra, a one man tour-de-force who (between cigarettes) will joke with the customers in any number of languages. I've heard it said there are many women in his life, but whatever his personal arrangements may involve, he's a terrific cook, his Paupiette de Sole and Salad de Gambas having finally earned him a place in the Guide Gault-Millau.

The dining room once formed part of an ancient abbey, but greeting you these days at the entrance is a suit of armour holding a spear – something

Signor Balistra has been known to brandish at the customers. Outside, tables block the street, where at the end of the evening the tired chef will surface from below stairs, sometimes with a bottle of Marc under his arm, for a quiet chat about what you've eaten. Then one sees that behind the cheerful façade, there's a man who is as passionate about what he prepares as any of the highly paid superstars.

Which brings me back to the Forum and Van Gogh's café – or the restaurant on the floor above it, Le Vaccarès. The balcony offers a panoramic view of the square, which like the café is best experienced at night. Bernard Dumas cooks a varied menu based on local recipes, given extra zip thanks to his considerable skills. The set menu contains a warm Foie-Gras with Arlesienne Rice and a perfect Dorade Grillee with a reduced sauce of fennel, aubergine and garlic, similar to a Greek Scourdalia.

But on my last night in Arles I wasn't really concentrating on the food. A film crew had arrived at the Nord Pinus earlier on, and were disrupting traffic whilst discussing the next day's shoot in the middle of the road. (Give them the choice and a film crew will always choose the road rather than the pavement for a chat.) From the windows above, new faces looked down on the square, where waiters continued to dash between the parasols balancing trays filled with chips and beer.

One last 'tomate' and I was off. At the corner I turned to take a final look back. The short-order chef at the bar-tabac flicked a cigarette out of the upstairs window and another pretty girl danced beneath Mistral's statue, but this time it was me who was the centre of attention.

The mime artist was right behind me.

The Night Café, Place du Forum - Arles.

Café Combier

Saint-Rémy-de-Provence.

The bulls of the Camargue are the most noble of creatures, but to end life as a sausage strikes me as being a less than dignified manner in which to exit this world. However, as a small compensation they also form the main ingredient in another great regional favourite, the Gardiane – a delicious casserole that will also infuse the kitchen with the mouth-watering smells of Provence.

GARDIANE CAMARGUAIS (for 7 or 8 people)

5lbs of stewing steak, cut in 3 inch pieces
6 garlic cloves, peeled and left whole • 4 onions, thinly sliced
8 medium sized carrots, cut in 3 inch ovals
2 sticks of celery, cut in ½ inch slices • A bottle of hearty red wine
4 tablespoons of olive oil • 1 large sprig of thyme
A small handful of rosemary, finely chopped
2 bayleaves • 2 handfuls of black, oil-preserved olives • Salt and pepper

The day before, put the meat, garlic, onions, carrots and celery in a bowl. Pour over the wine and leave to marinate for 24 hours. Drain the meat and heat the oil in a casserole. Fry the meat until brown, add the herbs and olives, and season with salt and pepper. Pour in the marinade and bring to the boil, turning the meat thoroughly. Cover and simmer for about 2 hours, adding more wine if necessary. To be authentic, serve with plain boiled rice.

Strictly speaking, Nice is the rightful home of the Pan Bagnat, but this appetizing sandwich is popular all along the Cote d'Azur where it remains the quintessential seaside bite. This simple recipe (if you can call it that) was given to me many years ago by Patrick Boscq whose tiny restaurant in the perfume capital of Grasse specializes in traditional Provençale cuisine.

PAN BAGNAT (for 1 person)

1 French loaf • A simple vinaigrette dressing
1 small tin of tuna (in brine, not oil) drained and flaked
1 green pepper, halved and cut in ¼ inch slices
A small handful of black olives, stoned and halved
1 tin of anchovy fillets • Ground black pepper

Cut about 12 inches off the bread and slice almost in half, leaving it hinged along one edge. Dribble enough vinaigrette over the inside to make the bread moist. Spread the tuna over the bottom half and on top of this place the sliced green pepper and sprinkle with the olives. Lay 5 or 6 anchovy fillets diagonally across, add pepper and squeeze firmly together. This sandwich tastes especially good accompanied by a couple of hard-boiled eggs and a bottle of beer.

I stood staring at the empty building. A gnarled trunk wound upwards from its wrought-iron porch, disappearing under a cascade of bougainvillaea that overgrew the six tall windows. A line of plane trees cast dappled light on the dilapidated outbuildings, where a half hidden cement mixer showed scant evidence of repair work long overdue.

It was 2.30 on a still afternoon, the time when all over France shutters remain shut, streets are deserted, and romantic idiots like me find themselves dreaming of transforming run-down hovels into Michelin starred hotels. Still, at a million-and-a-half francs it looked a bargain from where I stood, staring at the fuzzy print in the estate agent's window.

It seems only yesterday I stood outside a similar window thinking the same thoughts, in the same town. In fact, nearly thirty years have passed.

A French girl had invited me to spend a few weeks in Cannes, staying at the roof-top apartment of a relative, who during the summer worked as a croupier at the casino in Monte-Carlo. It was my first time in France, arriving late at

Le Marché Forville — Cannes.

night and with no idea of what lay in store for me the following morning.

Pulling back the shutters, I was hit by warmth from the bluest sky I'd ever seen. And the view! Every house had a terrace on top, where people sat in bamboo chairs, eating croissants and reading coloured newspapers, and the smell of coffee was everywhere.

I was sent next door to buy a loaf of bread, and for the first time set foot in a boulangerie. Above the noise of hooting cars and whining bicyclettes, frantic announcements echoed from a thousand transistors tuned to Radio Monte-Carlo.

Later on, I walked down the Boulevard Carnot and down the steps into the market. The Marché Forville is held undercover in a huge car park, every morning except Mondays, and seven days a week from June to September. It's devoted entirely to food, and is where the Bacon restaurant in Antibes gets its fish, so you know the quality.

I think one of life's greatest pleasures is to wander aimlessly up and down the aisles of places like this. Harrods couldn't hope to match the variety of what's on show between the pillars of this wonderful market; the largest tomatoes and the tiniest radishes, rock-hard garlic and the softest mushrooms; celery as tall as trees and leeks as thin and delicate as church candles.

Mountains of langoustine grapple with crabs and lobsters on tables buried in an avalanche of crushed ice. Sea urchins dare you to take a poke, and gold-flecked rougets look like they've just this minute flipped out of the net to take a closer look at you.

Rickety hand-carts are wheeled in and out, constantly replenishing the stalls, and waiters balancing tin trays dash back and forth from surrounding bars,

constantly replenishing the stallholders. Because of the market, many old cafés still survive, and where the Rue Louis Blanc slopes down to meet the Rue Felix Faure, right on the corner is Chez Astoux, or to give it its full name, Astoux et Brun. The decor isn't much smarter than a transport café's, yet on a summer's evening you find local families rubbing shoulders with the filthy rich across the pavement tables.

By the kerb, a stall sells oysters, mussels and anything else with a shell on, and traffic comes to a stand-still as cars are left with doors wide open and engines running while their owners nip out to pick up their pre-arranged orders.

In the winter it's equally chaotic inside, waiters whip out corks as fast as they prise open the oysters and the formica walls drip with condensation from the steaming tank of Soupe de Poissons. I once watched an old lady, dressed all in black, plough her way through a Plateau des Fruits de Mer the size of a dustbin lid. The more she ate, the more visible she became behind the tray, but they'd forgotten to include the cork, stuck with pins to extract the winkles. Not bothering to attract attention, she calmly removed the pin from her hat and methodically continued with her lunch.

Chez Astoux was a later discovery, but on my first morning in Cannes, having found the market, I went off in search of more. It wasn't long before I was standing in a pedestrian street, buzzing with life and rich with the smells of roast chicken and pizza.

The Rue Meynadier must be one of the busiest streets in Provence, jammed with patisseries, boucheries and fromageries, some considered to be the best in the South of France. Many are open-fronted, hence the smells, and shop-keepers are genuinely friendly, keen for you to sample things and happy to answer questions at great length, never mind how long the queue is.

It's a crazy street. In one shop you find beautiful cuts of meat, larded ready for the oven, yet next door they're selling shoes you wouldn't be seen dead in. At another, the pastries will leave you drooling, whilst opposite on display are suits you only ever see worn by the man who reads the weather forecast.

At the bottom end there's a fromagerie called La Ferme Savoyarde, and the cheese-boards of many a fine restaurant are made up of varieties supplied by Monsieur Ceneri. I don't know what you call the cheese equivalent of a sommelier, but he's it, and La Ferme Savoyarde is his cellar.

Nosing your way along the shelves is like studying an Ordnance Survey of France; Epoisses from Burgundy, Cantal from the Auvergne; tangy Bleu de Sassenage from the Dauphine and red-orange Munster from the slopes of Alsace-Lorraine.

Imagine living in a place where in order to get the best food, you only have to walk down a single street. Fancy some pasta? Call in at no. 31. At Aux Bons Raviolis, Signor Foppiani will offer you pasta filled with crab, asparagus and half-a-million

other things. Perhaps a joint of Charolais beef or some herb-fed lamb from the Sisteron hills? It's not for nothing the picture in the window of no. 38 shows Georges Brugère shaking hands with our own Queen Mum. If you like your lamb 'en croute', stop at no. 50, where Chiania stock flour by the sack-load. And how about a nice rhubarb tart to finish? Ernest at no. 53 has just baked the best one in the world.

It was on this first holiday that I received an invitation to the Cannes Film Festival, which surprisingly, given the prestige of the event, arrived in the form of a leaflet pushed through the letterbox. Understanding little French, it took some time before I realized the invite was, in fact, to view the winning entries in the Cannes *Amateur* Film Festival. Nevertheless, it was being held at the same venue and offered a chance to see the old Palais des Festivals from the inside. (Even in 1966 there were rumours concerning its future.)

The night we went I couldn't help noticing Dirk Bogarde seemed to be absent, nor was Robert Mitchum dancing for photographers at the water's edge. The topless girls I'd seen pictured arm in arm with Eddie Constantine were also missing. In fact, there was nobody there at all. Inside, things were slightly more active. We were given numbered seats along with about sixty others, most of whom were entrants in the competition. As most seats remained empty I failed to understand why we were asked to move on no less than three occasions, but after an hour's delay the show began.

We stuck it for the best part of two hours, until the projector ground to a halt, the lights came on and then went off again, leaving the audience

literally in the dark as to what was going on. Up to this point my money was on a film called **Winter Walks**, consisting of unrelated footage of various alpine locations, interrupted at the end of each scene by a woman wearing a red anorak, nervously entering the frame with her hand glued to her brow, surveying the landscape. At the point of cutting to the next scene she'd

turn to camera and in extreme close-up treat the viewer to a smile so manic that nearly thirty years later it still gives me the creeps.

Instilled with the magic of the movies, we fumbled our way out onto the Croisette and into the Blue Bar. This place holds premier position from which to view the evening activities along this sumptuous boulevard and for which, of course, you pay a premium. Likewise, Côte d'Azur Cars have a fleet made up entirely of Porsches, so you can cruise up and down the Croisette observing the antics outside the Blue Bar, for which you also pay a premium. People watching people … watching people.

Though not really known for its food, beneath all the nonsense the Blue Bar wasn't at all bad. I had lunch here once out of season. The Foie-gras was excellent and the Moules à la Poulette was true to the recipe, flavoured with mushroom stock and then thickened with egg yolks. I remember leaving thinking just how pleasant Cannes is, off-peak. The sun still turns the gulf of La Napoule the palest shade of emerald, and waiters, relieved of the summer madness, become human once again.

Near the port, people play boules under trees that hide the awful reincarnation of the festival building and also in the Place de l'Etang, a pretty lamp-lit square close to the Pointe de la Croisette. Maybe things have changed, but games played here were never what you'd call sporting; serious money changed hands between some pretty desperate looking people. Quite often the police would arrive and cart them off, still arguing amongst themselves, only for another game to start as soon as they'd gone.

There used to be a café here, similar in feel to the old Café des Arts in St-Tropez, with a vast seating area outside. It was run (or so I thought), by a very tall man with a chalky complexion, his black hair greased flat across a huge forehead, and known to everyone as 'Frankenstein'. Each night he'd be there in his dinner suit, passing among the tables, stopping every so often to enquire after peoples' health or if the service was up to scratch. It turned out he had nothing whatsoever to do with the place, but simply enjoyed playing the part of the sympathetic host, which the management happily allowed him to do.

L'accès à la plage est interdit aux chiens

Casualty – Boulevard de la Croisette – Cannes.

Cannes is full of smart shops. On the Croisette itself there are two famous jewellers, Cartier and Van Cleef & Arpels. (This was the branch Lino Ventura robbed in *La Bonne Année*.) At the very beginning of the Rue d'Antibes is a gunsmith's called Calvin Giraud. Its windows are very Bond Street in appearance, but the contents would be more at home in a black museum. There's a star shaped instrument about the size of a beer mat, its points honed razor-sharp, which is hurled through the air at some unsuspecting prey. There's also a device made of cheese wire, like the one used by Robert Shaw in *From Russia With Love*. Perhaps some gourmet has discovered that the flesh of a wild boar is more tender if you leap out from behind a tree and garrotte it.

Anyway, this is the best shop in Provence to buy a set of boules, and everything connected with the game. Expandable rulers with retractable tips for measuring hairline distances, magnets on strings, so players with back problems can retrieve their boules without bending, and pocket 'marqueurs' for those too drunk to keep score.

It's also the only place I know still making the traditional leather sacks, hand stitched, with brass buckles, in which to carry your boules.

Between the Pointe de la Croisette and Juan-les-Pins is a narrow beach dotted with huts selling the ubiquitous Pan Bagnat. This is Golfe-Juan, and side by side are two restaurants that have been going since the 20s, both little more than a couple of long wooden cabins. One's called Nounou and the other Tetou, and each year they compete for pole position in the guides.

There's something about Nounou I've always preferred, but inside, they're both spotless, like grand dining cars derailed at the water's edge. Each has its own bit of beach, and there's no better way to eat fish than with the sound of the ocean lapping close to your table. At Tetou,

the Soupe de Poissons is a bit richer than most, but at both, the fish is superb. You either grill a sea bass properly or you don't. At Nounou they stuff it with fennel branches before grilling, infusing it with a delicate aniseed flavour, and serve it very simply with melted butter and plain steamed potatoes.

I love the way this restaurant changes, depending on the time of day. At lunchtime it's like a smart trawler, in the evening, you're on board a luxury liner – and when French women dress up they really know how. During summer, every designer-name in the book is paraded up and down the centre cat-walk.

If the film festival is on, from nearby tables you hear in advance who's definitely won this or that award (always wrong), how attempts have been made to nobble the jury chairman (often right), and that naturally, the final ceremony will be a total fiasco (always right).

What you'll never hear, is anything whatsoever to do with what's going on in the outside world.